MARVEL

SPIDEY
and his AMAZING FRIENDS

CAN YOU SPOT IT?

AUTUMN PUBLISHING

MARVEL
SPIDEY
and his AMAZING FRIENDS

TEAM SPIDEY NEEDS YOUR HELP TO STOP THE BAD GUYS AND SAVE THE DAY!

Use your super searching and spotting skills to uncover hidden objects and characters on each page.

Once you've found everything, fill in your own Super Hero profile as the newest member of Team Spidey!

A WALL OF WEBS

Spin has trapped Rhino with his webs, but the villain is trying to escape. Can you find five broken webs like the ones above, so that Spin can repair them?

SPIDEY

Real Name: Peter Parker

Bio: After Peter Parker was bitten by a radioactive spider, he became the friendly neighbourhood Spider-Man! Peter loves science, and he uses his smarts to invent things like his web-shooters. He also solves problems, and that's what makes him such a great leader of Team Spidey! He always tries to do the right thing and protect people. Spidey knows that with great power comes great responsibility.

POWERS AND ABILITIES

- Wall-crawling
- Spidey-Sense
- Custom-built web-shooters
- Superhuman agility, strength and speed
- Genius-level intellect
- Invention skills

BADGE BUSTER

Look at this jumble of badges.
Can you find eight Spidey logo badges?

TENTACLE TANGLE

Team Spidey are trapped in Doc Ock's terrible tentacles! Can you find and rescue everyone in time?

GHOST-SPIDER

Real Name: Gwen Stacy

Bio: Ghost-Spider is the coolest hero around! When she's not playing the drums, she's out with the Spidey Team doing her best to protect the city from bad guys. Her detective skills are second-to-none, and she's the best at being sneaky. Just like the rest of the Spidey Team, she'll never give up until all the villains are brought to justice. There's no outsmarting Ghost-Spider!

POWERS AND ABILITIES

Wall-crawling
Spidey-Sense
Superhuman agility, strength and speed
Web-wing gliding
Detective skills
Custom-built web-shooters

PUMPKIN PRANKS

Green Goblin has set a pumpkin prank trap. Find Peter, Miles and Gwen before time runs out and the pumpkin pranks explode!

A TOTAL CAT-ASTROPHE

Bootsie is always getting herself into trouble!
She's hiding in this pile of tennis balls.
Can you help Peter find his cat five times?

SPIN

Real Name: Miles Morales

Bio: The youngest member of Team Spidey, Miles is enthusiastic and fun. He loves to paint and draw almost as much as he loves being a hero! Along with the rest of Team Spidey, Miles uses his powers to protect the city and stop the bad guys. Miles can turn invisible with his cloaking ability and even use his Arachno-sting to put villains to sleep. He might be new to being a hero, but Miles is an expert at having fun!

POWERS AND ABILITIES

Aerial spin manoeuvre
Wall-crawling
Spidey-Sense
Superhuman agility, strength and speed
Cloaking
Arachno-sting

ROBOT RUMBLE

Doc Ock's Octobots are on the loose!
Find TRACE-E, TWIRL-E and TWIST-E to
rescue them from the robots' metallic claws.

HIDDEN AMONG HEROES

Team Spidey are hanging out with their Super Hero friends, but the bad guys are planning on spoiling the party. Can you help Team Spidey spot Doc Ock, Green Goblin, Rhino and Electro?

SUPER HERO NAME:

· ·

Real Name: · · · · · · · · · · · · · ·

Bio: · · · · · · · · · · · · · · · · · · ·

· ·

· ·

· ·

· ·

· ·

DRAW YOUR OWN SPIDEY SUPER HERO SUIT!

POWERS AND ABILITIES

· ·

· ·

· ·